COVER:

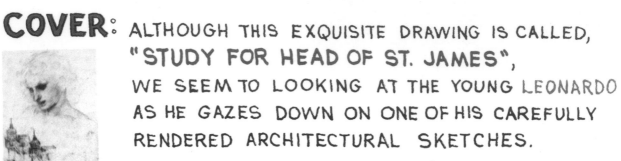

ALTHOUGH THIS EXQUISITE DRAWING IS CALLED, "STUDY FOR HEAD OF ST. JAMES", WE SEEM TO LOOKING AT THE YOUNG LEONARDO AS HE GAZES DOWN ON ONE OF HIS CAREFULLY RENDERED ARCHITECTURAL SKETCHES.

ROYAL LIBRARY, WINDSOR

THE DRAWING OF THE YOUTHFUL HEAD COMBINES LEONARDO'S FREEDOM OF LINE AND PERFECTION OF SHADING. HE SHOWS THE PRECISION OF A SUPERB **DRAFTSMAN** IN HIS DETAIL OF THE CASTLE TOWERS.

BESIDES BEING A GIFTED PIONEER IN THE FIELDS OF BOTH ART AND SCIENCE, LEONARDO WAS AN ACCOMPLISHED HORSEMAN WHO LOVED TO DRAW HORSES, AN INSPIRED NATURALIST WHO COLLECTED BATS, WASPS AND LIZARDS, AND AN EXCELLENT MUSICIAN.

SOME 10,000 DRAWINGS FROM LEONARDO'S MANY SKETCH BOOKS ARE SEEN IN MUSEUMS THROUGHOUT THE WORLD.

STUDIES OF HORSES   ROYAL COLLECTION, WINDSOR

HEAD OF HORSE   ROYAL COLLECTION, WINDSOR

DETAIL: THE ANNUNCIATION   UFFIZI GALLERY, FLORENCE

DEDICATED TO KATE STEINITZ, AN ARTIST AND FRIEND
WHO HAS SPENT MANY OF HER 81 YEARS SHARING
HER KNOWLEDGE AND LOVE FOR LEONARDO DA VINCI
WITH THE WORLD.

WORLD RIGHTS RESERVED BY ERNEST RABOFF AND GEMINI SMITH, INC.

LIBRARY OF CONGRESS CATALOGUE CARD NO. 78-139054

ISBN TRADE : 0-385-07738-6
LIBRARY : 0-385-02438-X
PRINTED IN JAPAN BY TOPPAN

LEONARDO DA VINCI

By Ernest Raboff

ART FOR CHILDREN

A GEMINI SMITH BOOK

EDITED BY BRADLEY SMITH

PUBLISHED BY
DOUBLEDAY & CO., INC.

GARDEN CITY, NEW YORK

LEONARDO DA VINCI WAS BORN

ON APRIL 15, 1452 IN THE MOUNTAIN VILLAGE OF VINCI IN CENTRAL ITALY. HIS FATHER, SER PIERO DA VINCI (DA MEANS FROM) WAS A SUCCESSFUL LAWYER WHO SOON MOVED TO FLORENCE WHERE HE WAS EMPLOYED BY THE RULING MEDICI FAMILY.

AT THE AGE OF 17 LEONARDO WAS ALREADY KNOWN AS A BRILLIANT, CLEAR THINKING, ABLE YOUTH. HIS GREATEST INTERESTS WERE MUSIC, SCULPTURE AND DRAWING. REALIZING HIS SON'S UNUSUAL TALENT, HIS FATHER SHOWED LEONARDO'S DRAWINGS TO ANDREA DEL VERROCCHIO, A WELL-KNOWN SCULPTOR, GOLDSMITH AND PAINTER. FOR THE NEXT SEVEN YEARS THE YOUTH STUDIED AND WORKED WITH HIM. IN ADDITION TO PAINTING THE YOUNG ARTIST STUDIED ARCHITECTURE, GEOMETRY AND ENGINEERING.

IN HIS LONG AND USEFUL LIFE LEONARDO WAS BOTH FRIEND AND TEACHER TO

ARTISTS, APPRENTICES, SCIENTISTS, KINGS, POPES and SCHOLARS WHO SOUGHT HIM TO TALK AND TO LEARN.

ONE OF THE MOST TALENTED MEN OF ALL TIME, LEONARDO DIED ON MAY 2, 1519.
FRANCIS , THE KING OF FRANCE, SAID THAT NO MAN KNEW AS MUCH AS LEONARDO DA VINCI.

PORTRAIT OF DA VINCI BY ERNEST RABOFF

LEONARDO DA VINCI WAS A PAINTER,

SCULPTOR, PHILOSOPHER, INVENTOR, WRITER, ARCHITECT, BOTANIST, BIOLOGIST, CITY-PLANNER, AERODYNAMIC AND HYDRAULIC ENGINEER, PHILOLOGIST, MUSICIAN, PHYSIOLOGIST AND MATHEMATICIAN. LEONARDO BELIEVED THAT ART

WAS A MAJOR PATH TO KNOWLEDGE.

LEONARDO WROTE: "ONE CAN HAVE NO GREATER AND NO LESSER MASTERY THAN ONE HAS OVER ONESELF."

"NO HUMAN INVESTIGATION CAN BE CALLED TRUE SCIENCE WITHOUT GOING THROUGH MATHEMATICAL TESTS."

"EXPERIENCE HAS BEEN THE MISTRESS OF THOSE WHO HAVE WRITTEN WELL."

"TRUTH
IS SO EXCELLENT
THAT IF IT
BUT PRAISES
SMALL THINGS
THEY BECOME
NOBLE."

SELF-PORTRAIT   ROYAL LIBRARY, TURIN

"THE LADY WITH THE ERMINE" GIVES THREE EXCITING AND CREATIVE EXAMPLES OF LEONARDO'S PURSUIT OF KNOWLEDGE IN THE STUDY OF PORTRAITURE, ANATOMY AND COMPOSITION.

THE SENSITIVE FACE OF THE LADY, THE DRAWING OF HER HAND AND THE RENDERING OF THE ANIMAL AMAZE US WITH THEIR NEAR PERFECTION.

STUDIES OF TWO CHILDREN KISSING ROYAL COLLECTION, WINDSOR

STUDY OF CLASPED HANDS   WINDSOR

DA VINCI WAS THE FIRST PAINTER TO COMPOSE HIS WORK USING THE MATHEMATICAL PROPORTIONS AND THE ARCHITECTURAL STRENGTH OF THE PYRAMID AS A BASIS OF DESIGN.

THE LADY'S FOREARMS, HOLDING THE ERMINE, ARE THE BASE OF THE PYRAMID. HER UPPER ARMS AND THE LINES EXTENDING FROM HER SHOULDERS TO THE TOP OF HER HEAD FORM THE SIDES.

MICHELANGELO AND RAPHAEL ADOPTED SOME OF LEONARDO DA VINCI'S PRINCIPLES AND USED THEM IN THEIR OWN WORKS.

ROBINIA   ROYAL COLLECTION, WINDSOR

THE LADY WITH THE ERMINE   CZARTORYSKI MUSEUM, CRACOW

IN THIS DETAIL FROM "THE LADY WITH THE ERMINE" WE
FIRST NOTICE HER BEAUTY. THEN WE SEE HER CHARACTER
EMERGE AS LEONARDO PAINTS HER WITH CLASSICAL INSIGHT.
HE MAKES HER **BROWN** EYES SPARKLE WITH INTELLIGENCE.
BY SOFTLY LAYING ON ALMOST TRANSPARENT LAYERS OF
PAINT HE MAKES HER RADIANT SKIN SEEM REAL.

THE MASTERY OF DESIGN IS SHOWN IN THE CIRCLES,
LINES AND PLANES OF THE TWO ORNATE CORDS THAT
CROSS THE MODEL'S BARE FOREHEAD. THE SENSE OF DESIGN
IS FURTHER HEIGHTENED BY THE CURVE OF HER HAIR AS IT
FRAMES HER FACE.

TO FURTHER CONTAIN HER BEAUTY LEONARDO HAS CARE-
FULLY DETAILED HER NECKLACE.

ALTHOUGH LEONARDO DA VINCI NEVER MARRIED,
HIS PAINTINGS OF WOMEN REVEAL HIS ADMIRATION AND
SENSITIVITY TOWARDS THEM.

METHOD FOR WALKING ON WATER

PORTRAIT OF MASSIMILIANO SFORZA
PINACOTECA AMBROSIANA, MILAN

STUDY OF LIFE PRESERVER

DETAIL: THE LADY WITH THE ERMINE CZARTORYSKI MUSEUM, CRACOW

LEONARDO'S LOVE OF ANIMALS IS APPARENT IN
THIS PLEASING DETAIL FROM "THE LADY WITH THE ERMINE".

ALTHOUGH THE ARTIST MAGICALLY CAPTURED THE GRACE
AND LOVELINESS OF THIS FINE FURRED MEMBER OF THE
MINK FAMILY, HE ALSO WAS VERY
CAREFUL TO PAINT THE MUSCLE AND
BONE STRUCTURE OF THE ERMINE
WITH SCIENTIFIC ACCURACY AND
KNOWLEDGE. HE PAINTED THE PAWS
AND THE CLAWS WITH THE SAME
PATIENCE HE USED TO PAINT THE
FINE WHISKERS AND THE TUFTS OF
HAIR NEAR THE EARS.

FOLLY   ROYAL COLLECTION, WINDSOR

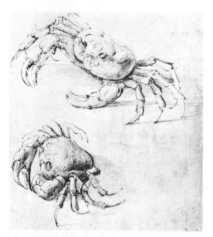

THE CRAB   WALLRAF-RICHARTZ MUSEUM, COLOGNE

NOTICE HOW THE WHITE HAIRS
OF THE ANIMAL'S COAT PICK UP AND
REFLECT THE COLORS OF THE LADY'S
CLOTHES AND SKIN.

THE EYES OF THE PET AND THE EYES
OF THE LADY ARE EQUALLY ALIVE.
AND SEEM TO BE INTERESTED IN
WATCHING THE ARTIST AT WORK.

THE MOUSE AND THE CAT   ROYAL COLLECTION, WINDSOR

LEONARDO KNEW THAT EYES
COULD BE TELESCOPES AND MICROSCOPES
WHEN ONE LEARNS TO USE THEM.

DETAIL: THE LADY WITH THE ERMINE   CZARTORYSKI MUSEUM, CRACOW

THE "MONA LISA", ALSO CALLED "LA GIOCONDA" IS THE MOST FAMOUS PORTRAIT IN THE WORLD. NOW CRACKED AND FADED BY TIME, IT WAS ORIGINALLY PAINTED SO DELICATELY AS TO SHOW EVERY EYELASH.

EVERYONE WHO HAS LOOKED UPON HER FACE HAS TRIED TO UNDERSTAND THE SECRET OF THE EXPRESSION IN THE EYES AND IN THE SOFT SMILE ON THE LIPS OF THIS MONA LISA.

IT IS AS THOUGH LEONARDO'S THOUGHTS ABOUT THE MYSTERIES OF WOMEN ARE WRITTEN IN THE REVEALING LINES, WARM COLORS AND DELICATE FORMS OF THIS GREAT PAINTING.

THERE IS A FEELING OF BEING CONTENT WITH THE WORLD IN THE QUIET BEAUTY OF THIS HANDSOME WOMAN.

THE BACKGROUND, WITH IT'S WINDING ROADWAY, SOFTLY ARCHED BRIDGE AND HIGH MOUNTAINS, ADDS TO THE RIDDLE OF THIS DA VINCI MASTERPIECE.

MONA LISA   THE LOUVRE, PARIS

IN THIS DETAIL OF THE
MONA LISA WE CAN STUDY
MORE CAREFULLY THE EXPRESSION
IN THE EYES AND ON THE LIPS.

THE LADY'S CHEEKS, ROSY, ROUND AND SOFT
SEEM TO TELL US THAT BENEATH HER
QUESTIONING GAZE LIES A READINESS
TO ACCEPT AND TO LOVE ALL MANKIND.

HER MOUTH, WITH ITS FULL LIPS AND
INWARD TURNING SMILE, CONTINUES
THE QUESTIONING OF HER EYES.

HEAD OF CHILD   UFFIZI GALLERY, FLORENCE

WITHOUT RICH ADORNMENT
HER PLAIN HAIR, UNORNAMENTED
NECK AND ERECT POSTURE CONVEY
A FEELING OF ROYALTY

LEONARDO PAINTED
THE BEAUTIFUL MONA LISA
MORE THAN 450 YEARS AGO.

POSTURES OF BABIES, STUDIES FOR FRESCO
ROYAL COLLECTION, WINDSOR

BECAUSE OF HIS GENIUS
SHE HAS BECOME THE BEST KNOWN
WOMAN IN THE HISTORY OF ART.

DETAIL: MONA LISA   THE LOUVRE, PARIS

"ST. ANNE, THE VIRGIN AND THE INFANT CHRIST WITH A LAMB" TELLS A STORY OF THE CHRIST CHILD, HIS MOTHER AND ST. ANNE, HIS GRANDMOTHER.

LEONARDO, INSTEAD OF PAINTING A RELIGIOUS SCENE, HAS USED THE CHARACTERS FROM THE BIBLE TO REPRESENT ALL GRANDMOTHERS WITH CHILD AND GRANDCHILD.

THE DESIGN IS A BOLD ONE WITH THE FOUR FIGURES RELATED TO ONE ANOTHER BY THE LONG SWEEPING CURVE THAT EXTENDS FROM ST. ANNE'S HEAD TO THE GRACEFUL ARC OF THE VIRGIN'S ARM AND THE CHILD'S ARM HOLDING THE LAMB.

IN THE SETTING OF THE PAINTING LEONARDO THE SCIENTIST HAS JOINED LEONARDO THE ARTIST. THE PEBBLES AT THE FEET OF THE VIRGIN AND THE STRUCTURE OF THE ROCKY LEDGE ARE SO FINELY PAINTED THAT THE SHAPE OF EACH ROCK CAN BE CLEARLY SEEN.

THE RED-BROWN EARTH AND FOLIAGED TREE ARE SEPARATED FROM THE SKY AND THE MYSTERIOUS MOUNTAINS IN THE BACKGROUND LIKE HEAVEN FROM EARTH.

DRAWING FOR ST. ANNE   THE LOUVRE, PARIS

KNEELING WOMAN   BRITISH MUSEUM

ST. ANNE, THE VIRGIN AND THE INFANT CHRIST WITH A LAMB   THE LOUVRE, PARIS

FEMININE HEADDRESS   ROYAL COLL., WINDSOR

THIS CLOSE-UP DETAIL OF ST. ANNE AND THE VIRGIN SHOWS ST. ANNE LOOKING LOVINGLY ON HER DAUGHTER. HER INWARD SMILE, HINTING OF SECRECY, IS MUCH LIKE THAT OF THE MONA LISA.

LEONARDO WARMLY SHOWS HOW A MOTHER'S LOVE CONTINUES AFTER HER CHILDREN ARE GROWN AND HAVE CHILDREN OF THEIR OWN. HER HALF-CLOSED EYES SEEM TO BE LOOKING BACK IN HER MEMORIES AND SEEING MARY AS A CHILD.

YOUNG WOMAN   FORMER ROYAL COLLECTION, TURIN

AS ST. ANNE REFLECTS FONDLY ON HER DAUGHTER, MARY REGARDS HER SON WITH A LOOK THAT ALL PARENTS AND CHILDREN WILL RECOGNIZE.

FOR MANY YEARS ART CRITICS THOUGHT THAT THIS WORK MIGHT HAVE BEEN PAINTED BY ANOTHER ARTIST, BUT BECAUSE OF THE SOFT TEXTURE OF THE PAINT AS IT WAS CAREFULLY APPLIED, THE SMILE OF ST. ANNE AND THE TRANSPARENCY OF THE FLESH TONES, ART EXPERTS NOW AGREE THAT IT COULD ONLY HAVE COME FROM THE HAND AND THE MIND OF LEONARDO DA VINCI.

DETAIL: ST. ANNE, THE VIRGIN AND THE INFANT CHRIST WITH A LAMB   THE LOUVRE, PARIS

THE INFANT FIGURE IN "ST. ANNE, THE VIRGIN AND THE INFANT CHRIST WITH A LAMB" IS SEPARATED BY AN ARM'S LENGTH FROM THE MOTHER AND GRANDMOTHER.

IN THIS WAY LEONARDO EFFECTIVELY DIVIDES THE ATTENTION BETWEEN THE TWO WOMEN AND THE BOY.

THE CHILD HAS LOOKED UP FROM HIS POSITION AT HIS MOTHER'S FEET. HE SEEMS TO BE SHOWING HER WHAT FUN HE IS HAVING WITH THE ANIMAL AND ASKING FOR HER APPROVAL

THE DOG AND THE FLEA   ROYAL COLL., WINDSOR

DA VINCI REPEATS THE TIGHTLY CURLED ROLLS OF HAIR ON THE INFANT CHRIST'S HEAD WITH THE LOOPED FLEECE COVERING THE LAMB.
FOR THE ARTIST, THE CHILD IS ALSO A LAMB.

LEONARDO DA VINCI WROTE: "A GREAT LOVE SPRINGS FROM A DEEP KNOWLEDGE OF THE THING ONE LOVES."

ASS AND OX   ROYAL COLLECTION, WINDSOR

DETAIL: ST. ANNE, THE VIRGIN AND THE INFANT CHRIST WITH A LAMB   THE LOUVRE, PARIS

CAPS AND HELMETS   ROYAL COLL., WINDSOR

STUDY OF PEASANT DIGGING   ROYAL COLL., WINDSOR

IN THIS "PORTRAIT OF A MUSICIAN" LEONARDO'S ORDERLINESS OF MIND AND ATTENTION TO DETAIL SHOW US AS MUCH ABOUT THE ARTIST AS ABOUT THE MODEL.

HE HAS PAINTED MORE THAN A LIKENESS OF THIS ATTENTIVE MUSICIAN, HE HAS SHOWN THE MUSICIAN'S DEDICATION TO HIS WORK, HIS RESPECTED PLACE IN SOCIETY AND HIS STRENGTH OF CHARACTER.

THE FACE AND THE SLENDER FINGERS HOLDING THE SHEET OF MUSIC GLOW WITH EQUAL WARMTH AND DRAW OUR EYES UP AND AROUND THE PAINTING.

PERHAPS LEONARDO IS SHOWING US THAT WE CAN LEARN MUCH ABOUT A PERSON IF WE OBSERVE THE HANDS AS WELL AS THE FACE.

STUDIES OF HEADS   FORMER ROYAL COLLECTION, TURIN

PORTRAIT OF A MUSICIAN   PINACOTECA AMBROSIANA, MILAN

DRAWING FOR ST. ANNE

PROFILE OF YOUTH   ROYAL COLL., WINDSOR

LEONARDO'S "FEMALE PORTRAIT" IS A PAINTING IN WHICH EVERY DETAIL IS EXCITING TO EXPLORE.

THE WOMAN'S FACE, SHAPED ALMOST LIKE A TRIANGLE BY THE CAREFULLY STYLED HAIR, HOLDS OUR ATTENTION WITH ITS STRAIGHT FORWARD GAZE.

HER EXPRESSION IS ONE OF THOUGHTFULNESS AND HER EYES ALMOST SEEM TO BE LOOKING INWARD RATHER THAN AT US.

WHAT PATIENCE AND CARE ARE NECESSARY TO PAINT SUCH FINE CURLS AND GLOWING HAIR. NOTICE THE SIMPLE ROLLED SCARF BINDING THE HAIR IN BACK, THE DARK VELVET AROUND HER NECK, THE WHITE BLOUSE AND THE GOLD-EMBROIDERED RED DRESS WITH LACED BODICE.

IN THE BACKGROUND, WE CAN SEE EACH DETAILED LEAF, THE REFLECTING POND AND THE CITY'S PALE DOMES AND SPIRES AGAINST THE STILL SKY.

FEMALE PORTRAIT   NATIONAL GALLERY, WASHINGTON

GROUP OF DANCERS FOR ALLEGORICAL COMPOSITION   ACADEMY, VENICE

"PORTRAIT OF A YOUNG WOMAN" GAVE LEONARDO AN OPPORTUNITY TO PAINT MANY OF THE THINGS THAT FASCINATED HIM ALL HIS LIFE.

HE DID NOT LOOK FOR BEAUTIFUL MODELS BUT RATHER FOR UNUSUAL AND INTERESTING FACES. HE WAS MASTER OF THE PORTRAIT NO ARTIST OF HIS TIME, AND FEW SINCE, UNDERSTOOD THE PAINTING OF LIGHT AND SHADOW ON THE HUMAN FACE SO WELL.

FROM THE TIME OF HIS CHILDHOOD LEONARDO LOVED TO DRAW KNOTS AND IN THIS PORTRAIT HE HAS PAINTED AT LEAST 63 SMALL KNOTS, ONE LARGE ONE AND A LOOPED GOLD CHAIN.

BUT IT IS NOT THE LUMINOUS PEARLS, THE RICHLY COLORED JEWELS NOR THE ORNATE HEADDRESS OF HIS MODEL, BUT THE IMMORTAL LEONARDO SPIRIT THAT MAKES THIS PORTRAIT A GREAT WORK OF ART

IN "THE ANNUNCIATION" THE ANGEL IS ANNOUNCING TO MARY THAT SHE WILL BECOME THE MOTHER OF THE CHRIST CHILD.

LEONARDO HAS USED THIS THEME TO CREATE A MYSTICAL SCENE OF QUIET AND POETIC BEAUTY IN THE KIND OF SETTING HE LOVED TO PAINT.

THE COLORFULLY DETAILED CARPET OF FLOWERS IN THE FOREGROUND FORMS A BASE UPON WHICH THE ANGEL KNEELS. THE GRACEFUL FOLDS OF HER GARMENT ALMOST MOVE IN THE GENTLE BREEZE.

LEONARDO HAS FOUND A PLACE FOR HIS KNOWLEDGE OF ANATOMY IN THE PAINTING OF MARY AND THE ANGEL, FOR HIS PERCEPTION OF BOTANY IN THE PLANTS AND FLOWERS AND FOR ARCHITECTURE IN THE SPIRED CITY IN THE BACKGROUND.

EVEN THE SCALLOP SHELL ON THE CARVED END OF THE TABLE IS IN PERFECT HARMONY WITH THE TOTAL DESIGN OF THE PAINTING.

HEAD AND SHOULDERS OF WARRIOR IN PROFILE
BRITISH MUSEUM

MOST CRITICS BELIEVE THIS SCENE WAS PAINTED WHEN LEONARDO WAS BETWEEN 20 AND 23 YEARS OF AGE WHILE HE WAS STILL A STUDENT IN THE STUDIO OF THE GREAT VERROCCHIO

DETAIL

COMPLETE PAINTING: THE ANNUNCIATION   UFFIZI GALLERY, FLORENCE

STUDIES AND POSITIONS OF CATS   ROYAL COLLECTION, WINDSOR